# TIMELESS LONDON

# TIMELESS LONDON

## Robert Franklin

CHARTWELL
BOOKS, INC.

This edition published in 2007 by

# CHARTWELL BOOKS, INC.
A Division of
## BOOK SALES, INC.
114 Northfield Avenue
Edison, New Jersey 08837

ISBN-13: 978-0-7858-2337-7
ISBN-10: 0-7858-2337-9

© 2007 Compendium Publishing, 43 Frith Street, London,
Soho, W1D 4SA, United Kingdom

Cataloging-in-Publication data is available from the Library
of Congress

Printed and bound in China

Design: Ian Hughes/Compendium Design

Page 2: Designed in 1848 by Astronomer Royal Sir George Airey, the Great
Clock at the Houses of Parliament first chimed the "Big Ben" bell in 1859.
Page 4: Harrod's first opened its famous doors in 1849. At that time it was
housed in a single room and employed two assistants. Over the following
decades it grew into the world's best-known department store.

# Contents

# Introduction

Situated on the banks of the River Thames, in the heart of Westminster, the Houses of Parliament are the seat of national government for the United Kingdom.

# Introduction

London is the capital city of England and the United Kingdom of Great Britain and Northern Ireland. Built around the River Thames the city covers 620 square miles and is home to a population of over seven million people. The metropolis that began as an outpost of the ancient Roman Empire grew over the centuries to become the thriving center of the British Empire, which at the height of its power covered over a quarter of the world's land surface.

There is little or no archaeological evidence to suggest that there was any significant permanent settlement in the area of modern day London prior to the Roman invasion in AD 43 that was led by the Emperor Claudius. The Romans built a bridge across the River Thames (remains of which have recently been discovered not far from the site of the modern London Bridge) and soon a thriving settlement named *Londinium* was established on the north bank. In AD 61 the nascent town was razed to the ground by the Iceni tribe, led by Boudicea who had been flogged and forced to watch the rape of her daughters by the Romans. The Iceni uprising was soon quashed and *Londinium* was rebuilt and continued to prosper, eventually replacing Colchester as the capital of Roman Britain. In around AD 200 the Romans built a defensive wall around the city. Some portions are still visible in London today and the wall's boundaries outline the present-day financial district, known as "the City." *Londinium* thrived under Roman rule for another 200 years but by the fifth century the Roman Empire in the West was in terminal decline and in AD 410 the last Roman troops were withdrawn and the city's fortunes plummeted.

At the height of its Roman occupation over 40,000 people had inhabited London, but in the years following its abandonment this figure fell dramatically and large areas of the city fell into ruin. However, by the seventh century the city was slowly beginning to expand again. Following the conversion of the East Saxon King Sebert to Christianity the first cathedral dedicated to Saint Paul was built in the early 600s.

During the eighth and ninth centuries London re-established its position as an important center for trade and began to flourish once more. This newfound prosperity and the town's strategic location soon brought London to the attention of the Danish kings who were raiding along the east coast of England at this time. Numerous raids were launched up the River Thames and in 851 the city was once again razed to the ground. The exact events of the following decades are now largely lost to us, but what is known is that in the century that followed London was rebuilt and changed hands between the Danes and the English in a merry-go-round of invasion and occupation.

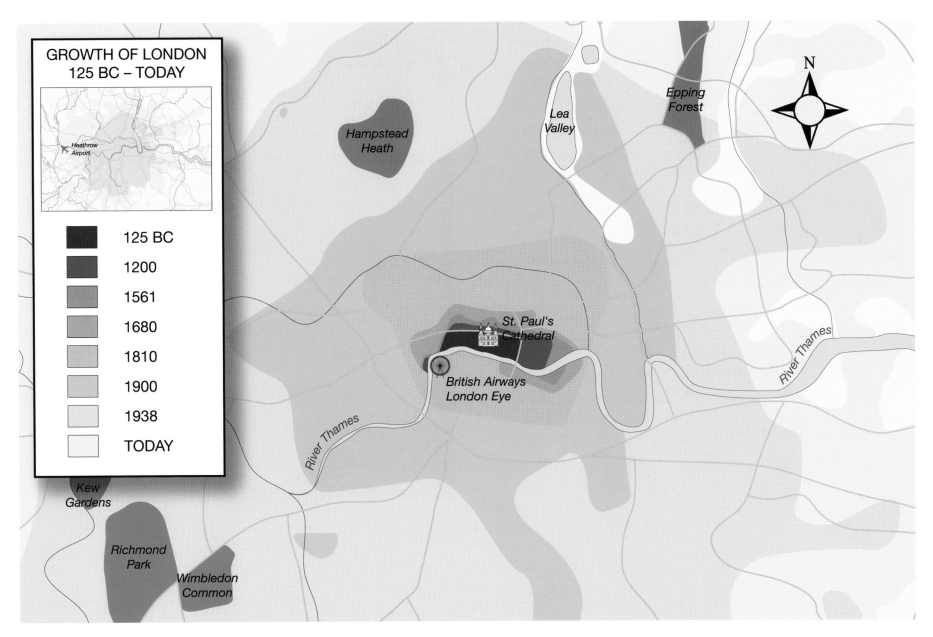

GROWTH OF LONDON
125 BC – TODAY

Heathrow Airport

125 BC
1200
1561
1680
1810
1900
1938
TODAY

Hampstead Heath

Lea Valley

Epping Forest

N

St. Paul's Cathedral

River Thames

British Airways London Eye

River Thames

River Thames

Kew Gardens

Richmond Park

Wimbledon Common

Stability was established during the reign of the Danish king Cnut (also known as Canute) who came to power in 1017 and with peace came a return of prosperity. On his death Cnut was succeeded by the devout English king Edward the Confessor, who began construction of a huge abbey at Westminster that was consecrated in December 1065.

On Edward's death the line of succession was unclear; both Edward's cousin, Duke William of Normandy, and his brother-in-law, Harold Godwinson claimed the throne. The English chose Harold as their king and he was duly crowned in a ceremony at the newly finished Westminster Abbey. William was incensed by this decision, claiming that Edward had promised him the throne, and he gathered an army and launched an invasion. William defeated Harold at the Battle of Hastings on October 14, 1066 (an event celebrated in the famous Bayeux Tapestry) and was crowned King of England on Christmas Day 1066 in Westminster Abbey.

The reign of William the Conqueror marked both the start of the period of history known now as the Medieval (or Middle) Ages and set the tone for the future development of the city of London. Realising that he needed to rule by consent as well as by force, William granted a charter that upheld the rights previously enjoyed by the wealthy and influential citizens of London under Saxon rule. In return for taxes paid to the monarch, London maintained a degree of independence and self-governance. However the velvet glove did contain an iron fist and William also built a castle fortress in the southeast of the city as a symbol of his power. This was the first structure of the complex that

ABOVE: Discovered on a building site in the Southwark area of South London in 2002, this plaque bears an inscription with the oldest known Roman naming of the city of London.

RIGHT: A sixteenth century map of London, showing the City of London and the City of Westminster expanding out from the banks of the River Thames.

would later become the Tower of London. More construction began in 1097 under William's son, William Rufus, who commissioned the hall that would become the center of the Palace of Westminster, the main royal residence throughout Medieval times. At this time London was in a sense two separate cities, the City of Westminster was the center of the royal court and the seat of government while the City of London was the partly self-governed center of commercial activity.

Throughout the Middle Ages, London thrived and expanded and as it did so the influence and importance of the city and its institutions increased. Now a succession of monarchs found themselves forced to court favor with the guilds that virtually controlled London. In 1191, Richard I reconfirmed the right of the city to self-governance and in 1461 Edward IV gained the throne with the support of the London merchants. As trade flourished, markets that still exist today were established including the meat market at Smithfield and the fish market at Billingsgate. International trade also boomed and the Thames and its wharves teemed with ships carrying imported goods such as wine, spices, and precious metals from across Europe. Although the steady growth of the city brought great prosperity it also led to problems for its citizens. Because London had grown organically, rather than in a planned fashion, it had become a maze of narrow, winding streets with little or no sanitation. The consequence of this was frequent outbreaks of disease. In fact, between 1348 and the famous Great Plague of 1665 the city suffered from sixteen plague epidemics.

From 1455 to 1485 England was a battleground as the opposing forces of the House of Lancaster and the House of York fought out the War of the Roses for the English throne, but on August 22, 1485, the Lancastrian Henry Tudor defeated Richard III at the Battle of Bosworth, effectively bringing the war to an end. Henry reinforced his position by marrying Elizabeth of York and thereby reuniting the two royal houses. The combined red and white roses, the symbols of the two houses, became the emblem of the Tudor monarchy. Henry VII (as he became) established a merchant navy and commissioned the Henry VII Chapel in Westminster Abbey, but it was his son Henry VIII who was to have a truly long-lasting impact on the city of London.

By 1527, Henry VIII's first wife, Catherine of Aragon, had failed to produce the male heir that he was desperate for to continue the Tudor line. The king asked Pope Clement VII to annul the marriage, but his request was refused and this set in motion a chain of events that was to lead to great upheaval and lasting political and religious consequences in England. Henry's response was to sever England's ties with the Pope in Rome and to have himself declared the Supreme Head of the Church in England. The Reformation was to have a profound impact on the landscape of London. At that time the Catholic Church owned much of the property and land in the city and this was confiscated by the monarchy and redistributed to Henry's most valued supporters. Many religious buildings in London and throughout England were torn down completely.

The hugely unpopular Queen Mary temporarily returned England to Catholicism but this was widely resisted and the queen earned her nickname of "Bloody Mary" when she had 300 Protestants burned at the stake in Smithfield. Mary's reign was to last for just five years and when she was succeeded by her sister Elizabeth I in 1558. London was on the cusp of a Golden Age of discovery, expansion, and the arts.

By 1600 the population of London had risen to around 200,000 and during Elizabeth's reign the English navy, founded by Henry VIII, began to dominate the oceans. Francis Drake sailed around the world and was knighted upon his return; expeditions sailed to the newly discovered America and in 1588 Sir Walter Raleigh defeated the Spanish Armada of King Philip. Elizabethan London also saw the great age of English drama, the plays of William Shakespeare and Christopher Marlowe were written and performed in London during Elizabeth's reign and are still recognized as classics of English literature today.

Having never married or produced an heir, Elizabeth (known as the Virgin Queen) was the last of the Tudor monarchs; she was succeeded by the Stuart King James I. James's reign was almost cut short by the Gunpowder Plot of 1605 when Guy Fawkes and his fellow conspirators were caught attempting to blow up the Houses of Parliament. James was succeeded by his son Charles I in 1625, and despite opening Hyde Park to the public in 1637 Charles was an unpopular monarch, particularly in London. Following his attempt to enter Parliament in 1642 to arrest five members of the House of Commons on a charge of treason, the country was

This 1816 aquatint shows the current church of St. Martin-in-the-Fields in Trafalgar Square that was designed by James Gibbs and consecrated in 1726. There has been a church on the site since at least as early as 1222 when the first recorded mention is made of its existence.

plunged into a civil war between the Cavaliers (the supporters of the monarchy) and the Roundheads (the supporters of Parliament), led by Oliver Cromwell. London was almost universally on the side of the Roundheads but following their eventual victory and the beheading of Charles at Banqueting House on January 30, 1649, the city became a drab and dreary place. The Puritanical Protectorate established by Cromwell saw the closure of the theaters, the removal of the organs and choirs from churches, and even the banning of Christmas.

Such an austere rule could not last for long and in 1659 Cromwell's son Richard was forced to resign as Lord Protector. The

following year the exiled son of the executed King Charles I was crowned King Charles II amid much rejoicing in the streets of London. With the restoration of the monarchy London again became a vibrant and exciting capital; theaters were reopened and extensive building works were undertaken throughout the city. However Charles II's reign was to be blighted by two of the greatest tragedies to strike London. In 1665 a strain of plague so strong that it could kill within hours broke out in the city. The royal court and just about anyone else with the means to do so abandoned London. The eventual death toll for the Great Plague has been estimated as high as 100,000, at that time almost one third of the population of

the city. London was only just recovering from this calamity when on September 2, 1666, a fire broke out in Pudding Lane. The inferno swept through the city and raged for three days, destroying four-fifths of its buildings including over 13,000 houses and eighty-nine churches.

When London was rebuilt in the wake of the fire an Act of Parliament ensured that new buildings were constructed of brick or stone rather than the highly flammable wood that had previously been the used in the majority of construction work. Sir Christopher Wren was tasked with rebuilding many of the churches that had perished in the flames. The most famous of his

ABOVE: A 1909 view of Piccadilly Circus, the central point of London's West End Theaterland. Since its erection in 1892, the statue of Eros has been one of the most recognizable landmarks of the city and is frequently used as a meeting point for tourists and Londoners alike.

works, St Paul's Cathedral, remains one of the most iconic London buildings today.

Despite these twin catastrophes London continued to grow and by 1700 the population had risen to over half-a-million and the city was starting to overtake Amsterdam as the most important financial center in the world. The eighteenth and nineteenth

Originally known as the Empire Stadium when it was first built in 1923, Wembley Stadium was the home of the English football team for almost eighty years. It was here in 1966 that England won the soccer World Cup for the first and, so far, only time.

centuries saw London expanding at an incredible rate both in terms of buildings and population. By 1800, over a million people were living in the city and by 1900 this figure had risen to over six million. New bridges were built across the Thames, at Westminster in 1750 and Blackfriars in 1769. As the city expanded ever outward, the old Roman wall that had stood for centuries was torn down to allow traffic easier access to the city and areas that had once been outlying villages, such as Islington in the north and Battersea in the south, were swallowed up to become part of the now sprawling metropolis.

With size came grinding poverty in some areas, compounded by the age-old problem of sanitation, and crime was also rife on the streets. To answer at least one of these problems, in 1829 Sir Robert Peel created the Metropolitan Police Force in an attempt to establish law and order in the city. The officers were soon nicknamed "Peelers" or "Bobbies" for their founder (the latter remaining in common parlance to this day). Then, in the mid-nineteenth century, the problem of sanitation in London was finally addressed when Joseph Bazalgette oversaw the construction of underground sewers to carry the waste generated in London away from the city. Up until this time the river Thames had been the repository for much of the city's waste and was consequently little more than an open sewer. Following the opening of Bazalgette's sewers the incidences of disease, particularly cholera, in the city were greatly reduced.

As London entered the twentieth century, it was the thriving hub of an empire that stretched across the globe. The optimism

LEFT: A striking view of the damage inflicted on London during the Blitz of World War II. St. Paul's Cathedral, which can be seen dominating the skyline, miraculously managed to survive the bombings virtually unscathed and was a potent symbol of the indomitable "Blitz spirit" of the time.

and wealth of the great British Empire were demonstrated in the opening of fabulous new luxury hotels, department stores, and theaters in the capital. Although the effects on London of the First World War were far less dramatic than those of World War II, the city did experience its first taste of German bombing raids, carried out by Zeppelins. In all over 600 people were killed by the bombs.

The years between the two world wars were marked by great poverty during the Depression of the 1930s and by the rise of extreme political parties such as the British Union of Fascists led by the charismatic political chameleon Sir Oswald Mosley who had previously been both a Conservative and Labour Member of Parliament.

With the outbreak of World War II nearly two million of London's children were evacuated to the countryside due to the threat posed by the Luftwaffe. The bombing raids over London, known as "the Blitz", were at their most intense from September 1940 to May 1941, during which time over 18,000 tonnes of high explosives were dropped on the city destroying over a third of the City and the East End and killing over 30,000 Londoners.

In the years following the war, London initially struggled to recover, with housing being a major issue due to the destruction wrought by the Blitz. However, the city did manage to host the 1948 Olympics in Wembley Stadium during an otherwise bleak time. The skyline of the city was dramatically altered as high-rise

blocks of flats were built to alleviate the housing crisis though these were to prove unpopular with many residents. Nevertheless, by the mid-1950s the city was well on its way to recovery from the ravages of the war and there was a new air of optimism across the country leading the then Prime Minister, Harold Macmillan to claim that "most of our people have never had it so good."

Throughout the 1950s and 1960s London also witnessed a heavy influx of immigrants from old colonial countries such as India, Pakistan, and the Caribbean. From now on London would become a much more culturally diverse city than it had previously been. Unfortunately, the native Londoners did not always welcome these immigrants as demonstrated by the race riots of Notting Hill in 1958. Although the following decades saw much progress in race relations within the city, tension caused by economic as well as social factors still simmeried and there were further riots in Brixton during the 1980s. During the 1960s London was also at the center of the "Swinging Sixties" as the music and fashions of the city became worldwide phenomena. In 1969, the Rolling Stones played a free concert in Hyde Park and half-a-million people, equivalent to the entire population of London less than 300 years previously, attended the event.

The optimism and hedonism of the sixties gave way to the grim realities of the three-day week and the IRA bombing campaigns of the 1970s. However, as during the Blitz, Londoners refused to be cowed and the city slowly began to prosper again. During the 1980s the Docklands area that had been in decline since the 1960s became the subject of a huge regeneration project

LEFT: Old and new London cheek-by-jowl: the Victorian engineering masterpiece of Tower Bridge (left) spans the Thames next to the ultra-modern City Hall building (right) that houses the offices of the Mayor of London.

RIGHT: Since opening in 2000 as part of Britain's millennium celebrations, the London Eye has become one of the most popular tourist attractions in the world. A trip in one of the Eye's pods offers stunning panoramic views across and beyond the city of London.

and is now the site of some of the most sought after residential and commercial property in the city.

The twentieth century had been one of dramatic change for London, the old certainties of the empire were replaced by a new and less well ordered world in which both Britain and her capital have been forced to re-evaluate their place. However, the city entered the new millennium with a mood of optimism for the future. On July 6, 2005 London won the right to host the 2012 Olympics, making it the first city in the world to have hosted the games three times (having done so previously in 1908 and 1948) and providing huge boost to the city.

The very next day, July 7, 2005, the city was rocked by the terrorist bombings that struck at London's public transport network. Londoners reacted as they always have done to such adversity; they carried on with their normal daily lives, some sporting T-shirts with the message "Not Afraid" emblazoned on them.

London remains a vibrant city at the forefront of world affairs and is still hugely influential across a range of cultural fields such as music and fashion; it is also still the heart of the fourth largest economy in the world and attracts over thirteen million tourists every year.

# Roman Foundations to Tudor London: 43 AD–1557

This statue of Boudicea, who led the native revolt against the Romans, by Thomas Thornycroft, sits on the western side of Westminster Bridge, near the Houses of Parliament.

# Roman Foundations to Tudor London: 43 AD–1557

From its foundation by the Romans, London was an important nexus for commerce. Its riverside location allied to the network of roads that the Romans built, made it an ideal trading center and by the middle of the first century it had all the trappings of an important Roman outpost—a palace for the governor, an amphitheater, a bathouse, and a basilica (a mixture of town hall and courtroom) as well as a forum (the focal meeting place and market of the city).

Once the Romans left, the city fell into decline for a time, but its excellent location ensured that this could not last forever and by the ninth century London was once again an important trading center. With the arrival of William the Conqueror in 1066 London's position as the primary city in England was sealed; from this time onward the city would always be the base of the monarchy in England.

In 1381 Wat Tyler led the Peasants Revolt to London and though outright revolution was averted when Richard II, aged only fourteen, rode out to meet the rebels at Smithfield, the city was looted and many buildings set on fire. Almost a hundred years later, in 1476, a revolution of a very different kind began when William Caxton established the first printing press in England at Westminster. He printed over 100 books in his lifetime including Chaucer's *Canterbury Tales* and Malory's *Le Morte d'Arthur*.

By the time of "Bloody" Mary's death in 1558 London was already established as one of the most important and influential cities in the known world. Trade with Europe was flourishing and the merchant and professional navies, the basis of the empire that was to come, had been established.

RIGHT: A statue of the emperor Trajan standing in front of one of the few remaining sections of the Roman wall that surrounded the town of *Londinium*. The statue and wall are in the Tower Hill area of London.

BELOW: Seen here, the remains of an ancient Roman amphitheater that was discovered under the foundations of Guildhall and the nearby Church of St. Lawrence Jewry in London.

Construction of the Tower of London began following the Norman invasion of England; at the time of its completion in 1097 the four-turreted White Tower was the tallest building in London. For centuries the tower was used as a prison and has been the site of the incarceration of some of the most famous names in English history, including Sir Walter Raleigh and gunpowder plotter Guy Fawkes.

1502. P. Z. - THE TOWER OF LONDON.

Located just off Fleet Street, Temple Church was built by the Knights Templar and consecrated on February 10, 1185. The church is featured in William Shakespeare's *Henry VI* and more recently in the novel and film *The Da Vinci Code*.

503. P. Z. - WESTMINSTER ABBEY.

LEFT: The burial site of many of the kings of England as well as the location of every royal coronation since 1066, Westminster Abbey has played a unique role in English history. Edward the Confessor first constructed a stone abbey on the site in the mid-eleventh century. Very little of this original abbey survives in the modern building as in the thirteenth century Henry III had the abbey rebuilt in the prevalent Gothic style of the times. Over the centuries that followed, the abbey was added to by a succession of monarchs and it stands today as the most impressive example of medieval architecture in London.

RIGHT: Named after the lead-roofed mansion that once stood adjacent to it, Leadenhall Market has been the site of a food market since 1321. Horace Jones designed the current wrought iron and glass-roofed market in 1881.

LEFT: During the Medieval Ages, London was effectively run by the various guilds that controlled commerce in the city. Although each guild had its own hall there was also a common meeting place, Guildhall, which was built between 1411 and 1440. The building survives to this day following restoration work carried out after bomb damage sustained during World War II.

RIGHT: The hammerbeam roof of the Great Hall at Eltham Palace (one of the finest examples of its kind in England) was built during the reign of Edward IV between 1475–80. Eltham was a favorite royal home throughout Medieval times, but after Henry VIII's reign it fell out of favor and was slowly allowed to decline until it was bought in the 1930s by the wealthy philanthropist Stephen Courtauld who restored the Great Hall and built an Art Deco mansion adjacent to it.

Located on the south bank of the River Thames, Lambeth Palace has been the London residence of the Archbishop of Canterbury (the head of the Church of England) for over 800 years. The earliest parts of the remaining building, including the brick Tudor gatehouse seen here, date from the fifteenth century. Over the centuries it has been much restored, most recently in 1828 by Edward Blore.

LEFT: An eighteenth century picture of the buildings and grounds of Hampton Court, which was intended to serve as a riverside retreat for Cardinal Wolsey, the Archbishop of York during the reign of Henry VIII. However, in a bid to curry favor with the monarch Wolsey presented it to Henry in 1528. The palace was opened to the public in 1838 by Queen Victoria and remains a popular tourist destination to this day. One of the most popular attractions for visitors to Hampton Court is the famous hedge maze that was planted in the gardens in 1702.

RIGHT: This image shows the Tudor gatehouse of St. James's Palace in Pall Mall. The palace was built by Henry VIII between 1531 and 1536 and served as a royal residence for over 300 years. Although it has been the official residence of the monarch since Queen Victoria's time, the reigning sovereigns have preferred to live at Buckingham Palace.

# Elizabethan and Restoration London: 1558–1713

This seventeenth century view of the waterfront at Westminster by the Czech draughtsman and engraver Wenceslaus Hollar, shows Westminster Cathedral (right) and Westminster Hall (center), which is incorporated in the modern Houses of Parliament buildings. Parliament House (to the left) does not survive today.

# Elizabethan and Restoration London: 1558–1713

By the time Elizabeth came the throne, the monarchy in England was as firmly established as it had ever been and the country and its capital flourished during her rule. Sir Thomas Gresham founded the Royal Exchange in 1566 and this was to provide the basis for London's ascent as the commercial capital of the world.

The most significant cultural legacy of Elizabethan London is undoubtedly the body of work left behind by its dramatists, most notably the works of William Shakespeare. Ironically, although the theaters were immensely popular and Elizabeth herself enjoyed having plays staged for her at the Royal Court, the Corporation of London (run by the city's guilds) banned them from the city. Thus, the theaters moved south of the river to Southwark, an area outside the control of the Corporation. At that time Southwark was a bawdy area, home of brothels, bear-baiting, and cock-fighting arenas as well as the playhouses.

Elizabeth's successor, James I, was responsible for commissioning the revolutionary architect Inigo Jones to produce a number of buildings that are still an integral part of the landscape of London.

During the Civil War that erupted in the reign of Charles I, London was seen as a vital prize by both sides. However, the city's sympathies lay firmly with the Parliamentarian Roundheads and when Charles marched on the city he was forced to turn back without even engaging in battle, having been met at Turnham Green by a force twice the size of his own. Without control of the capital, Charles was doomed and he was eventually defeated and executed in London.

Although Roundhead victory in the English Civil War changed the face of British politics forever, the Puritanical regime of the Protectorate under Oliver Cromwell that followed was a joyless one and Londoners greeted the Restoration with open arms. This period in London's history is brought vividly to life in the diaries of Samuel Pepys who rose to become Chief Secretary to the Admiralty under King James II and was influential in the establishment on the British Civil Service.

RIGHT: An early sixteenth century sketch of London, showing the Fleet Street and Temple Bar districts of London as well as the River Thames.

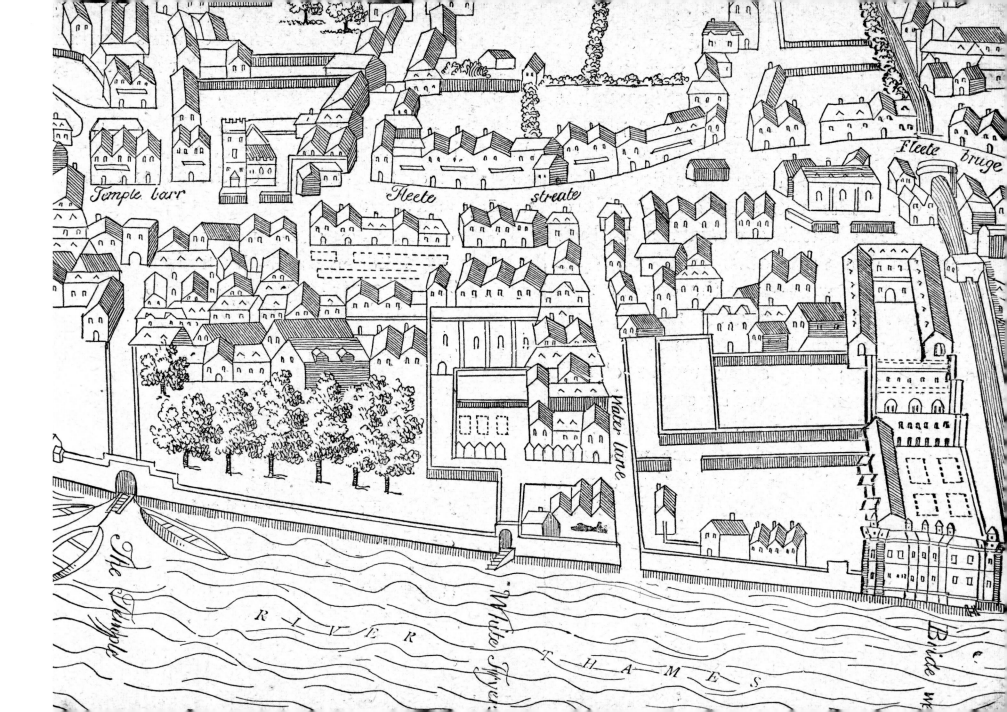

Temple barr

Fleete streate

Fleete bruge

Water lane

The Temple

White fryers

RIVER THAMES

Bride w

ABOVE: Middle Temple Hall, in the Inns of Court, took ten years to build and was completed in 1573. Although the hall is a dining facility for those studying law it also has a long history of entertaining debates and performances. In 1601 the first production of William Shakespeare's *Twelfth Night* was performed here.

ABOVE: Gray's Inn, another of the Inns of Court, was seriously damaged during the Blitz of World War II but has been largely restored. A sixteenth century wooden screen that survived thanks to having been dismantled for removal is still *in situ*. The gardens of the Inn were once a popular location for the staging of duels.

LEFT: The Globe Theatre in Southwark was built in 1599 to house the company of actors that included William Shakespeare. It burned down in 1613 and was rebuilt the following year, only to be closed in 1642 by the Puritans and finally demolished in 1644.

RIGHT: The Fortune Playhouse, with its resident company The Admiral's Men, was the main rival to the Globe. Like the Globe it was destroyed by fire (in 1621) and rebuilt. It too was closed by the Puritans and in 1661 it was torn down to be replaced by housing.

LEFT: Ham House in Richmond was built in 1610 for Sir Thomas Vavasour, who was Knight Marshal to James I. The house is now owned by the National Trust and visitors will find wonderful examples of lavish seventeenth century interiors as well as the formal gardens that were popular at the time.

RIGHT: The majestic Banqueting House in Whitehall was designed by Inigo Jones and was hugely influenced by his architectural studies in Italy. The building was completed in 1622 and contains a ceiling painting by Rubens that was commissioned by Charles I in 1630. It was the only building that survived the fire that destroyed Whitehall Palace in 1698.

LEFT: Another of Inigo Jones's masterpieces, Queens Chapel on Marlborough Road, was commissioned in 1623 by Charles I for his French wife, Henrietta Maria. Originally, the chapel was part of St. James's Palace, but following a fire in 1809 which destroyed the apartments that connected it to the palace and the construction of Marlborough Road in the 1850s it became separate from the palace.

RIGHT: Originally intended as a home for James I's wife, Anne of Denmark, Queen's House in Greenwich was completed in 1637. Unfortunately, Anne died before the house was finished, however it did become a favorite of Henrietta Maria, wife of Charles I. Following Henrietta's death, the house fell out of royal usage and more recently it has been opened as an art gallery displaying works from the collection of the National Maritime Museum.

ABOVE: Whether or not this is the same Old Curiosity Shop immortalized by Charles Dickens is unknown. However, what is certain is that it is one of the oldest (if not the oldest) shops in London and is one of the few buildings in central London to have survived the fire of 1666.

ABOVE: In 1666, soon after the threat of plague had receded, London suffered a further catastrophe when large sections of the city were destroyed by fire. This print of the Great Fire of London shows the ruins of a wall near Ludgate Prison, with Old St. Paul's Church and Old Bow Church in the background.

LEFT: A contemporary illustration showing the rich fleeing London to escape the bubonic plague that decimated the city's population in 1665.

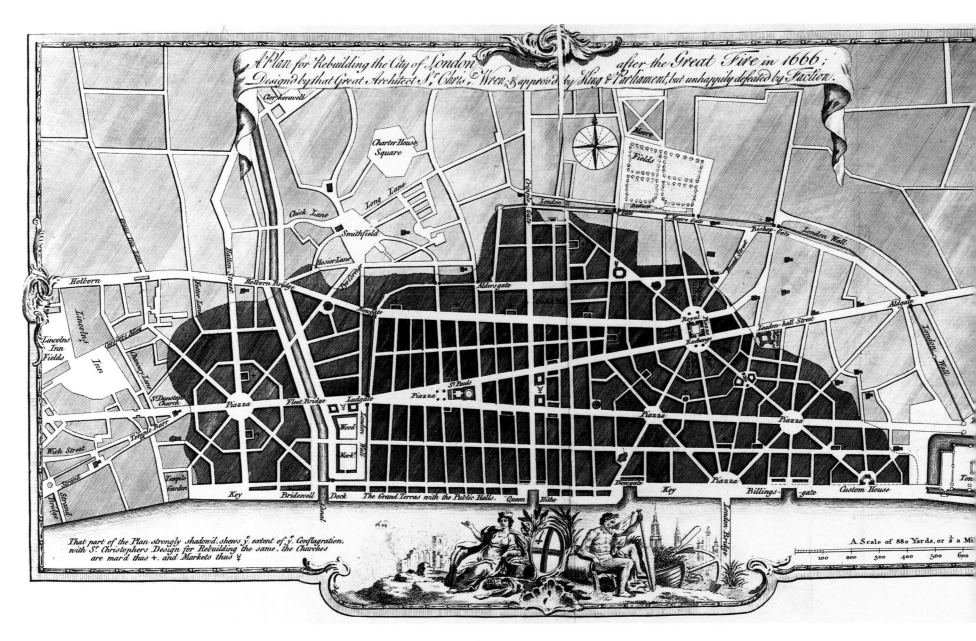

A Plan for Rebuilding the City of London after the Great Fire in 1666; Designd by that Great Architect Sr. Chris.r Wren; & approv'd by King & Parliament, but unhappily defeated by Faction.

That part of the Plan strongly shadow'd, shews ÿ extent of ÿ Conflagration, with Sr. Christophers Design for Rebuilding the same, the Churches are mar'd thus +. and Markets thus ✠

A Scale of 880 Yards, or ½ a Mile

LEFT: Christopher Wren's plan for rebuilding the City of London after the Great Fire in 1666. Although Wren is synonymous with the rebuilding of London, his plan to restructure the cities streets in a more ordered, grid-like pattern was not implemented.

RIGHT: Ye Olde Cheshire Cheese on Fleet Street is one of the few remaining traditional English pubs in London, with parts of the building dating back to the late seventeenth century. It has a strong literary association; past patrons include such luminaries as Samuel Pepys, Dr. Johnson, and Charles Dickens.

FOLLOWING PAGE: There has been a cathedral dedicated to St. Paul in London since the seventh century, but the current St. Paul's Cathedral is one of the most famous churches in the world. Designed by Sir Christopher Wren following the Great Fire of London, the cathedral took forty-five years to build, between 1675 and 1710, and remains one of London's best-loved monuments. It has been the scene of many important ceremonies, including the funerals of Lord Nelson and Sir Winston Churchill, Jubilee celebrations for Queen Victoria, and the wedding of Prince Charles and Lady Diana Spencer.

RIGHT: The oldest of the buildings of the Royal Observatory in Greenwich is Flamsteed House (named after the first Astronomer Royal, John Flamsteed) that was designed by Sir Christopher Wren and built in 1675–6. Further buildings, including the Meridian Building, were added during the eighteenth and nineteenth centuries. At the International Meridian Conference of 1884 in Washington, Greenwich was officially ratified as the internationally recognized site of the Prime Meridian, the imaginary line of zero longitude that separates the eastern and western hemispheres of the planet.

LEFT: The George Inn on Borough High Street is the only surviving example of the galleried coaching inns that were once common in London. The inn was rebuilt in 1676 following a fire that devastated the Southwark area. It is now owned by the National Trust and operates as a restaurant.

Right: British Prime Minister Tony Blair addressing the media outside no. 10 Downing Street following his victory in the 2005 elections. Only four of the houses built by Sir George Downing following his purchase of the land in 1680 remain. Number ten has been the official residence of the British Prime Minister since 1732, when it was given to the then incumbent Sir Robert Walpole by George II.

RIGHT: St. Clement Danes is located on a traffic island in the Strand. The church was designed in 1680 by Christopher Wren and takes its name from the original church on the site that was built by the descendants of Danish invaders. Currently, it serves as a church for the Royal Air Force.

LEFT: A royal procession leaves the gates of Buckingham Palace. The palace was originally built in 1702 as the London residence of the Duke of Buckingham whose son sold it to George III in 1761. The first monarch to take up residence in Buckingham Palace was Queen Victoria in 1837, since when it has served as both the royal home and the hub of monarchy's administration. Over the years the palace has been greatly altered and added to, most notably in the 1820s when George IV commissioned John Nash to add a new suite of rooms that doubled the size of the building. However, the front façade remains virtually the same as when it was first built.

# Georgian and Regency London: 1714–1836

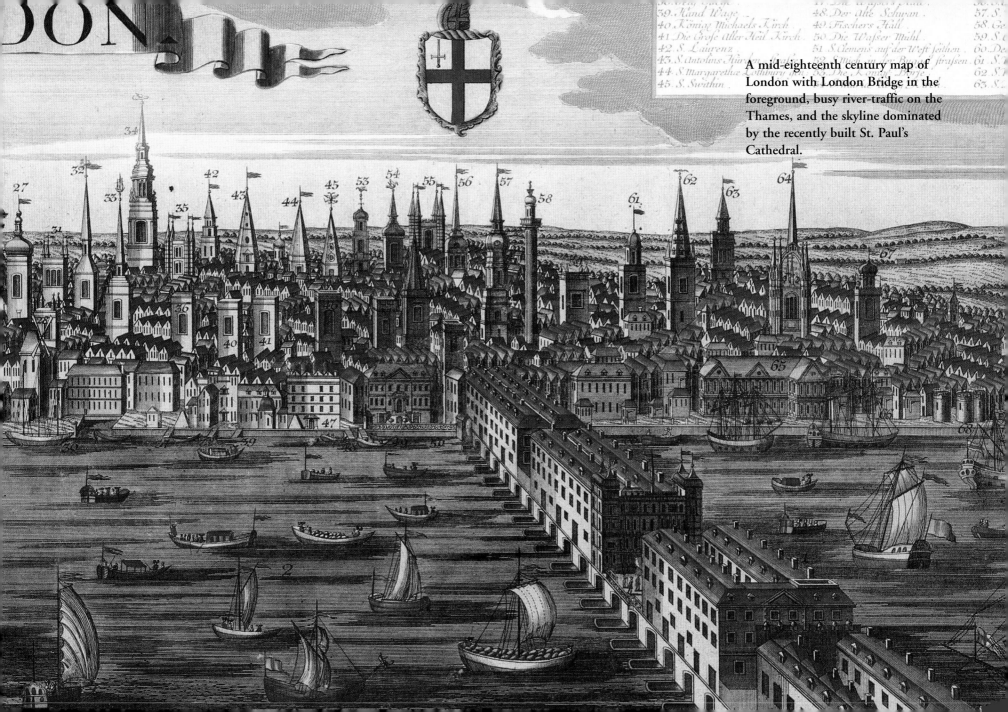

A mid-eighteenth century map of London with London Bridge in the foreground, busy river-traffic on the Thames, and the skyline dominated by the recently built St. Paul's Cathedral.

# Georgian and Regency London: 1714–1836

In Georgian times London began to take shape as the city we know today. New squares, such as Grosvenor Square and Berkeley Square, were laid out and rows of terraced houses sprang up in areas such as Mayfair and Soho. Fleet Street, which had originally been the road from the City of London to the City of Westminster, was established as the home of the newspaper industry that had evolved to cater for the increasingly literate population. The headquarters of the vast majority of national (and a great deal of local) newspapers remained in Fleet Street right up until the 1980s when there was an exodus to the newly redeveloped Docklands area.

One of the features of Georgian London were the coffee houses that abounded in the city. Although they had been present as early as 1650 in was in the eighteenth century that they became the hub of business and social activity. Indeed, two of the great London institutions were formed in coffee houses—the Stock Exchange began life in Jonathan's Coffeehouse in Change Alley and Lloyds on Lombard Street saw the founding of the Lloyds List in 1734.

During this period, the theaters once again found themselves at odds with the authorities when a series of political satires aimed at the First Lord of the Treasury, Robert Walpole, led to Parliament passing the Theatrical Licensing Act of 1737, which gave the Lord Chamberlain the power of censorship over all public theater performances. This draconian law had a huge effect on the type of plays that were written and performed subsequently and was only repealed in 1968.

By the end of the 1700s, the increase in commercial activity on the River Thames meant that the current docks were struggling to cope with their workload. Fearing that London would lose out to rival English ports, the city authorities embarked on a major dock-building exercise and by the end of the first decade of the nineteenth century the West India (1802), London (1805), and East India Docks (1806), had been built on the north side of the Thames, and the Commercial Dock (1809) on the south.

FAR RIGHT: Alfege is one of the most impressive of the churches designed by the Baroque architect Nicholas Hawksmoor. Located on Greenwich Church Street, the church was completed in 1714 and named for the Archbishop of Canterbury who was murdered by Danish raiders in 1012.

RIGHT: Although this house was built in the seventeenth century, its most famous inhabitant was Dr. Samuel Johnson who lived here between 1748 and 1759. It was here that Johnson compiled the first ever dictionary of the English language in 1755. The house is now open to the public and is decorated and furnished in the style of its eighteenth century heyday.

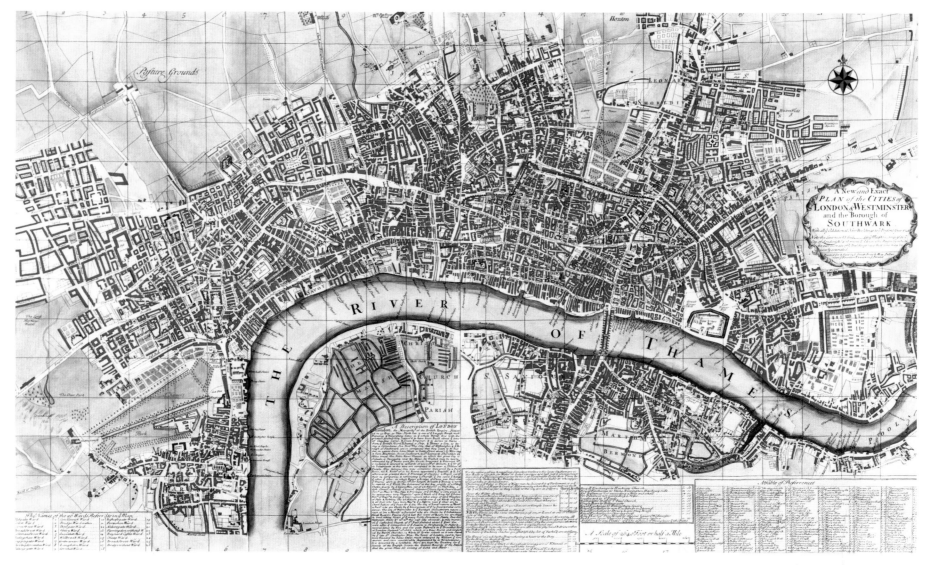

ABOVE: This 1724 map of London by Jan Kip shows the rebuilt city expanding out from the banks of the River Thames in the wake of the 1666 fire.

RIGHT: An early nineteenth century engraving of Mansion House, which was built in 1753. Designed by George Dance the Elder, the building is the official residence of the Lord Mayor.

A 1749 engraving of London Bridge and the surrounding area. Until 1750, this Medieval structure, lined with houses, was the only bridge to cross the Thames in London. It was replaced in 1831 by a bridge designed by John Rennie and completed by his son.

LEFT: Horse Guards in Whitehall was designed by William Kent and built in 1755. For many years this was the headquarters of the British Army. The building is still guarded by members of the Household Cavalry and is a popular tourist attraction.

The Earl of Mansfield, William Murray, bought the stately Kenwood House in Hampstead in 1754 and hired the architect and interior designer Robert Adam to remodel the house in 1764. In 1927, its then owner Lord Iveagh gifted it to the nation and since 1928 it has been open to the public, displaying a marvelous collection of Old Master paintings.

LEFT: The sumptuous interior of the Painted Room at Spencer House a magnificent house in St James's Place that was built in 1766 for the Earl of Spencer (an ancestor of Diana, Princess of Wales). Following an ambitious renovation, the house is now open to the public.

RIGHT: These terraced Georgian houses, built in the late 1700s, stand on the north side of Bedford Square, one of the best-preserved Georgian squares in the city.

Built in the 1770s, Somerset House on the Strand has in the past been the home of the Navy Board and the Inland Revenue, but these days it houses three art collections. Since 2000, the Somerset House Ice Rink has been enjoyed by thousands of skaters every winter.

ABOVE: Apsley House, on the southeast corner of Hyde Park, is another of Robert Adams creations. The building was designed for Baron Apsley and was constructed between 1771 and 1778. In 1807, the house came into the possession of the Wellesley family and was for many years the home of Arthur Wellesley, the Duke of Wellington, who defeated Napoleon at the Battle of Waterloo in 1815.

RIGHT: These buildings on the south side of Fitzroy Square were designed by Robert Adam and built in 1794. Both the south and the east sides of the square have survived virtually unchanged since they were originally built.

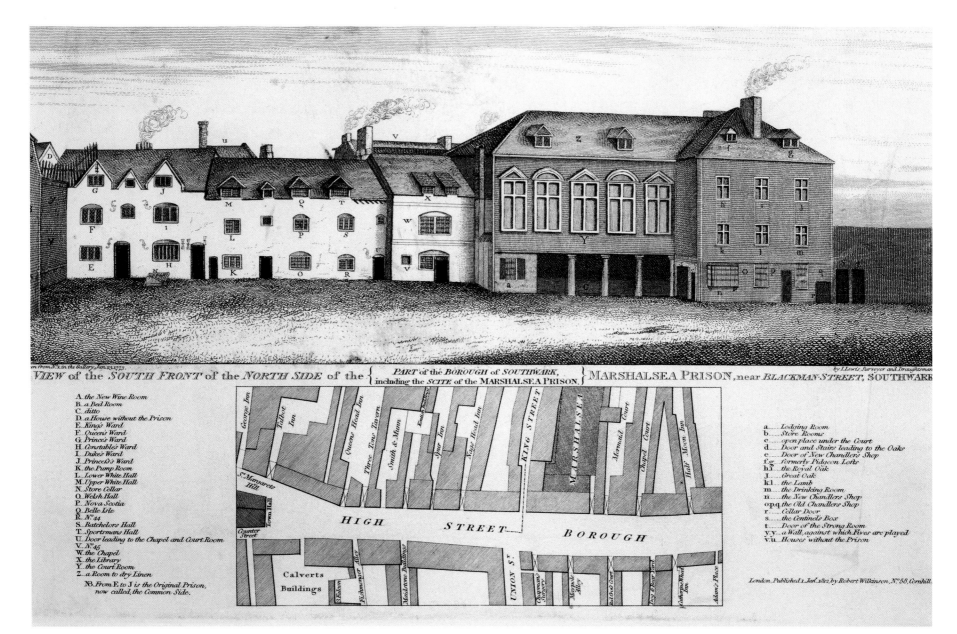

VIEW of the *SOUTH FRONT* of the *NORTH SIDE* of the { PART of the *BOROUGH* of *SOUTHWARK*, including the *SCITE* of the *MARSHALSEA PRISON*. } *MARSHALSEA PRISON*, near *BLACKMAN-STREET*, SOUTHWARK

A. the New Wine Room
B. a Bed Room
C. ditto
D. a House without the Prison
E. King's Ward
F. Queen's Ward
G. Prince's Ward
H. Constable's Ward
I. Duke's Ward
J. Princess's Ward
K. the Pump Room
L. Lower White Hall
M. Upper White Hall
N. Store Cellar
O. Welsh Hall
P. Nova Scotia
Q. Belle Isle
R. Nº 44
S. Batchelors Hall
T. Sportsmans Hall
U. Door leading to the Chapel and Court Room
V. Nº 45
W. the Chapel
X. the Library
Y. the Court Room
Z. a Room to dry Linen

N.B. From E. to J is the Original Prison, now called, the Common Side.

a. Lodging Room
b. Store Rooms
c. open place under the Court
d. Door and Stairs leading to the Oaks
e. Door of New Chandlers Shop
f.g. formerly Pidgeon Lofts
h.i. the Royal Oak
j. Great Oak
k.l. the Lamb
m. the Drinking Room
n. the New Chandlers Shop
o.p.q. the Old Chandlers Shop
r. Cellar Door
s. the Centinels Box
t. Door of the Strong Room
v.v. a Wall, against which Fives are played
v.u. Houses without the Prison

London Published 1 Janⁱ 1812, by Robert Wilkinson, Nº 58, Cornhill.

82

LEFT: A contemporary illustration of Marshalsea Prison in Southwark, one of the notorious debtors' prisons in London at the time. In 1824, Charles Dickens father, John, was incarcerated here and the prison is a central location in his novel *Little Doritt*. Marshalsea was demolished in 1849 and all that remains now is part of the inner wall.

RIGHT: The building that now houses the Imperial War Museum was built in 1811 and originally housed the Bethlehem Royal Hospital for the Insane, known as Bedlam. In 1930, the hospital moved from the premises and in 1936 the building was converted to house the museum that remains to this day.

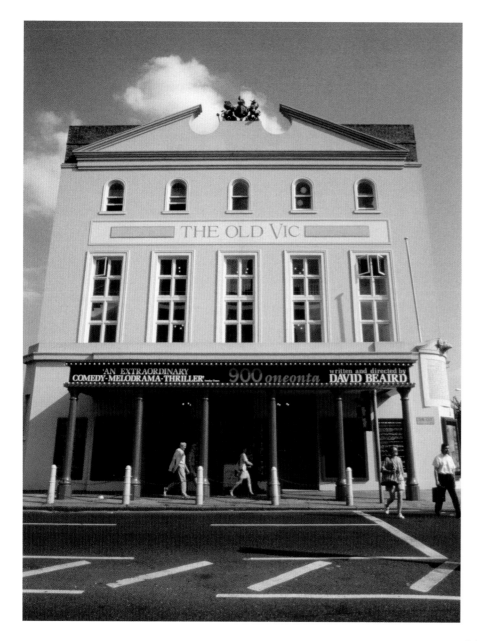

ABOVE: Considerably older than London itself, Cleopatra's Needle on the Embankment was gifted to Britain in 1819 by the Viceroy of Egypt. It is the twin of the similar monument in New York's Central Park.

LEFT: The Old Vic Theatre was built in 1818 and was originally known as the Royal Coburg Theatre—it was renamed the Royal Victoria in 1833. During the 1960s it became the home of the newly formed National Theatre and more recently it has had the Hollywood actor Kevin Spacey as its Artistic Director.

RIGHT: The regal front façade of the Theatre Royal Haymarket was designed by John Nash and built in 1821. In 1873, the Haymarket hosted the first ever matinée performance in a theater.

LEFT: The caryatids on the north and south sides of St. Pancras Parish Church are the embodiment of the ancient Greek inspiration for the building that was designed in 1822 by William Inwood and his son Henry. The architects based their design on the Temple of the Erectheum on the Acropolis in Athens.

RIGHT: Originally built in 1827 for William IV by John Nash, Clarence House is the official London residence of Prince Charles.

LEFT: This 1856 painting by James Pollard shows the Wellington Arch that was designed by Decimus Burton and built in 1828 on Hyde Park Corner. A sculpture by Adrian Jones was added to the top of the arch in 1912.

ABOVE: Designed by John Nash, Cumberland Terrace, on the east side of Regent's Park, is one of a number of terraces that surround the park. It was built in the late 1820s by William Mountford Nurse and named after the Duke of Cumberland, the younger brother of the king.

LEFT: In 1799, a competition was held for designs to replace the Medieval London Bridge that had been decaying for years. The engineer John Rennie won the competition and the bridge he designed is seen here on the occasion of its opening in August 1831. In 1968, the bridge was sold to the American entrepreneur Robert McCulloch who had it shipped to the U.S. where it was rebuilt at Lake Havasu City, Arizona.

LEFT: Although the oldest part of the Houses of Parliament (Westminster Hall) dates to 1097, the Gothic Revival structure that we know today was built between 1834 and 1870 following a fire that almost completely destroyed the old Palace of Westminster. The architect Sir Charles Barry, assisted by Augustus Welby Pugin, designed the new buildings, and one of the most famous features is the clock tower referred to as "Big Ben." In fact Big Ben is the name of the huge bell that was hung in the tower in 1858 and not the tower itself.

The National Gallery was founded in 1824 following the prompting of George IV. The main building that houses the gallery was designed by William Wilkins and was built between 1824 and 1828.

One of the great feats of engineering during Victorian times was the construction of the iron and glass Crystal Palace that was built in Hyde Park to house the Great Exhibition of 1851. Following the exhibition, the Crystal Palace was taken down and reconstructed at Sydenham Hill in South London where it remained until it was destroyed by a fire in 1936.

# Victorian London:
# 1837–1901

# Victorian London: 1837–1901

London was the largest and most populous city in the world during the reign of Queen Victoria and remained the political and financial capital of the globe until it began to be challenged by Paris and New York toward the end of the nineteenth century. Central to the growth and prosperity of the city were the advances in technology that had begun during the Industrial Revolution. The first public steam railway was built by George Stephenson in 1825 and by 1836 London had its first rail line linking London Bridge and Greenwich. By the middle of the century most of the major train stations in London had been built. Soon the whole country would be covered with a network of railways, drastically reducing travel times and signaling the beginning of the commuter era. The first underground line was opened in 1863, running from Paddington in the west to Farringdon in the east. By 1900, when the first Métro line in Paris opened, London already had a fully operational underground train network.

One of the great events of Victoria's reign was the Great Exhibition of 1851, held in Hyde Park. Championed by Prince Albert, this was the first of the great World's Fairs that were popular in the nineteenth and early twentieth centuries. Billed as a showcase of technology and manufacturing from around the world the exhibition was undoubtedly a chance for Britain to assert her prominence in these fields.

While Victorian London was certainly an exciting and wondrous city, it was also a metropolis of great contrasts. To be rich in London at this time was to live in the lap of luxury, but the poor lived in terrible conditions in slum areas such as Whitehall, which was terrorised by Jack the Ripper in 1888. The conditions suffered by the poor were highlighted in the novels of Charles Dickens and philanthropists such as George Peabody made some inroads toward alleviating the problems.

RIGHT: This photograph shows the spectacular atrium in Sir John Soane's Museum. In 1837, the renowned architect left his home to the nation on the condition that that it remain unchanged. Thanks to Soane, twenty-first century visitors are able to visit his home and view a wealth of memorabilia from the nineteenth century.

LEFT: One of London's most famous landmarks is Nelson's Column in the heart of Trafalgar Square. The monument was designed by William Railton and built between 1840 and 1843 to commemorate Admiral Horatio Nelson who died during the Battle of Trafalgar in 1805.

RIGHT: The current Royal Exchange building is the third to house the exchange that was founded by Sir Thomas Gresham in 1566. The previous two buildings were both destroyed by fire; the first in the Great Fire of 1666 and the second in 1838. The third building was designed by Sir William Tite and was officially opened by Queen Victoria in 1844. Currently, the Royal Exchange houses an upmarket shopping center.

LEFT: Sir Robert Smirke designed the main part of the British Museum in 1823, though it took until 1852 for construction of the buildings to be completed. The museum houses a wealth of artifacts from across the globe, the most famous being the Elgin Marbles from the Athenian Parthenon that were brought to Britain in 1806 by Thomas Bruce the seventh Earl of Elgin.

RIGHT: The Victoria and Albert Museum was founded in 1852 as the Museum of Manufacturers and was originally located in Marlborough House. It moved to its current location in 1857 and Sir Aston Webb designed the building that now houses the museum in 1899, the same year that it's name was changed to the Victoria and Albert Museum. The museum is dedicated to the decorative arts.

arches at Paddington train station. Isambard Kingdom Brunel designed the station with the assistance of the architect Sir Matthew Digby Wyatt and it was opened on January 16, 1854. When it was originally built the station contained three arches, the fourth being added during the enlargement of the station that took place between 1906 and 1915.

ABOVE: The Royal Opera House in Covent Garden is home to both the Royal Opera Company and the Royal Ballet Company. The present building, designed by E. M. Barry and built in 1858, is the third theater to stand on the site, the previous two having been destroyed by fire.

RIGHT: This 1860 map of the city shows how London had grown over the last century, with the boundaries of the city pushing outward both north and south of the River Thames.

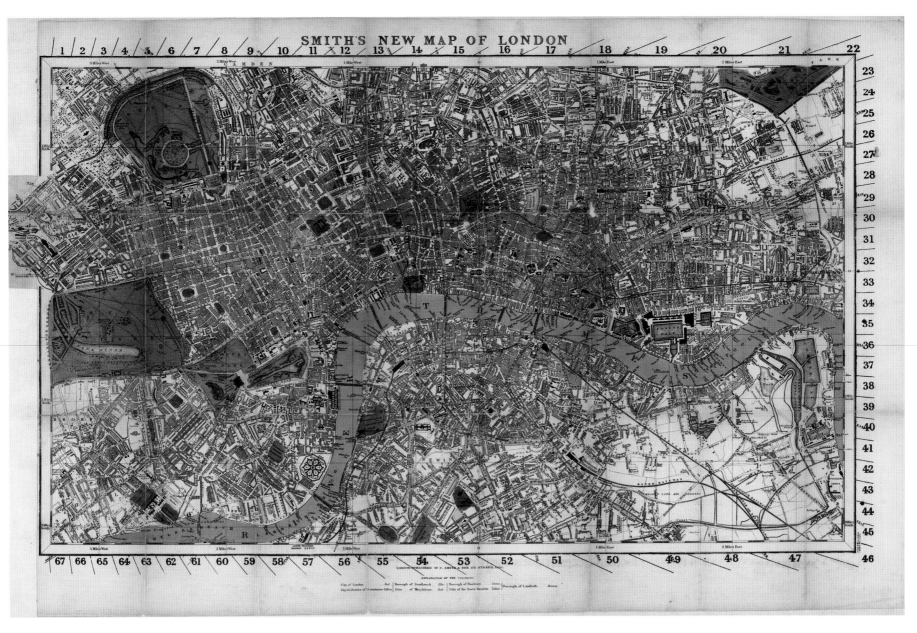

SMITH'S NEW MAP OF LONDON

The original Blackfriars Bridge, built in 1760, was demolished due to erosion in 1860. A new bridge (seen here) was built to the design of Joseph Cubbit and was officially opened by Queen Victoria on November 6, 1869.

Francis Fowke based his design for the Royal Albert Hall on the amphitheaters of Ancient Rome. Originally, the building was to be called the Hall of Arts and Science, but Queen Victoria renamed it in honor of her late husband. Opened in 1871, the Royal Albert Hall is most famous for the classical "Proms" concerts held here every year.

LEFT: While St. Pancras Station is undoubtedly one of the great feats of Victorian engineering, the majestic building at the front is in fact the Midland Grand Hotel designed by Sir George Gilbert Scott and opened in 1874. The hotel closed in 1935 and for most of the remainder of the twentieth century the building was used as offices. Currently it is undergoing a huge restoration.

RIGHT: Queen Victoria was heartbroken when her beloved husband Albert died aged only forty-one in 1861. This monument to his memory was designed by Sir George Gilbert Scott, with the statue by John Foley, and was completed in 1876.

The Natural History Museum in South Kensington was designed by Alfred Waterhouse and opened in 1881. The building itself is as impressive as the exhibits it contains. At the time it was built the techniques used in its construction were considered revolutionary and it remains as a remarkable example of Victorian ingenuity and inventiveness.

ABOVE: Completed in 1882, the Royal Courts of Justice in the Strand serve as the main civil courts for England and the massed ranks of the media can frequently be seen outside awaiting news of a verdict.

LEFT: The Brompton Oratory is one of London's most opulent Roman Catholic churches. Designed by Herbert Gribble, the main body of the church was built between 1880 and 1884 with construction of the dome being completed in 1896.

RIGHT: The Palace Theatre is one of the more impressive to be found along Shaftesbury Avenue. Built in 1891, it is currently owned by Andrew Lloyd Webber.

Completed in 1894, Tower Bridge is one of the most universally recognized symbols of London. Originally, the mechanism that powered the machinery that raises the bridge was steam driven, however in 1976 the system was converted to run on electricity.

RIGHT: Built on land that had previously been the site of a prison, Tate Britain opened in 1897 as the National Gallery of British Art. The art collector and sugar tycoon Henry Tate paid for the building and also donated his own collection to the gallery after which it became popularly known as the Tate Gallery. This name was officially endorsed in 1932, and since the opening of Tate Modern in 2000 it has been known as Tate Britain. The gallery is home to the largest collection of British art in the world.

ABOVE: The Temperate House at Kew Gardens (seen here) was completed in 1898 to house tender woody plants from the temperate areas of the world. On July 3, 2003, UNESCO officially made the Royal Botanic Gardens at Kew a World Heritage Site.

RIGHT: Founded in 1898 by the architect Charles Fitzroy Doll, the Russell Hotel in Bloomsbury, with its splendid mixture of Victorian and German Renaissance architecture, is one of the most impressive of the grand Victorian hotels still surviving in London.

# Early Twentieth Century: 1902–51

A view of Trafalgar Square in 1908 with the base of Nelson's Column in the foreground taken from the National Gallery.

# Early Twentieth Century: 1902–51

The first half of the twentieth century in London was dominated by the two world wars and the depression of the 1930s that separated them. However, prior to the outbreak of World War I the city continued its seemingly inexorable growth. Great civic buildings, such as Admiralty Arch, were erected, the first motorized bus services began in 1904, and in 1906 the first electric underground trains came into service.

While World War I is generally viewed as a soldiers' war it did have an impact on London. Not only was the city geared up to help with the war effort, but for the first time in centuries London actually came under attack: Zeppelin raids began in April 1915 and though they initially caused more alarm than damage, they eventually killed over 600 Londoners.

Following the war London's nightlife once again picked up and the "Roaring Twenties" saw nightclubs and dance halls spring up. However, the economic situation was still bleak for many and unemployment was high. In 1926 there was a General Strike that lasted for nine days and led to the army being used to help run the buses and the Underground.

Following the crash of the New York Stock Exchange in 1929 the situation worsened and by 1931 over three million people in Britain were unemployed. Despite this the population of London continued to rise significantly and by the time World War II broke out it was at an all time high of over 8.5 million (a level that it has yet to regain).

World War II was to have a far more devastating effect on London that the first conflict. The advances in flight technology meant that the German Luftwaffe was able to bomb the city almost every night for almost a year. London was subject to a blackout at night and when the air-raid sirens sounded, its citizens were forced to take shelter in the Underground stations and shelters across the city. The city emerged from the war partly in ruins.

RIGHT: An aerial view of Westminster Cathedral, the largest Roman Catholic church in England. Designed by John Francis Bentley and completed in 1903, the Byzantine-style cathedral is the seat of the Archbishop of Westminster and is the primary Catholic cathedral in England and Wales.

LEFT: Opened on the December 24, 1904, the London Coliseum is one of the largest theaters in the city. Until 1931 it was a variety theater, but following World War II it staged a number of big musical productions, such as *Guys and Dolls* and *Kiss Me Kate*. Since 1968 it has been the home of the English National Opera.

RIGHT: Commissioned by King Edward VII in memory of his mother Queen Victoria and designed by Sir Aston Webb, Admiralty Arch was completed in 1910. Situated at the entrance to the Mall it bears a Latin inscription that translates as, "In the tenth year of King Edward VII, to Queen Victoria, from most grateful citizens, 1910."

LEFT: With its distinctive dome, topped by a statue of Justice, the Old Bailey is one of the most famous criminal courts in the world. Although the site it occupies has been the location of London's foremost criminal court for well over 300 years, the present building was opened in 1907.

ABOVE: Seen here during the Remembrance Day service that is held every year on the Sunday nearest to November 11 (the date of Armistice Day, the anniversary of the official end of World War I), the Cenotaph in Whitehall was designed by Sir Edwin Luytens and erected in 1920 to honor the dead of World War I.

LEFT: Although it harks back to a much earlier age, the famous Tudor-style building that houses the Liberty store, designed by Edwin T. Hall and his son Edwin S. Hall, was in fact built in 1924 using wood from two ships, HMS *Impregnable* and HMS *Hindustan*.

RIGHT: Currently housing the headquarters of the BBC World Service, Bush House, on Aldwych, was originally built in 1935 by the American Irving T. Bush.

The Scotsman William Patterson
established the Bank of England in
1694. Originally, it was located in
Cheapside and later moved to
Princess Street. In 1734, it moved to
its present location on Threadneedle
Street. Sir Herbert Baker constructed
the current building between 1925
and 1939.

The Art Deco influenced Southgate Station on the Piccadilly Line section of the London Underground was designed by Charles Holden and opened on March 13, 1933. It is the most well known of the many Art Deco underground stations that were built around this time.

Located on the South Bank of the River Thames the Royal Festival Hall was both the first major public building to be constructed in London following World War II and the first post-war building to be made a Grade I listed building. Sir Leslie Martin and Sir Robert Matthew designed the unabashedly Modernist building and the Prime Minister Clement Atlee laid the foundation stone in 1949. Work was completed in 1951.

ROYAL FESTIVAL HALL

# Modern London: 1952–Today

A panoramic view of Canary Wharf, dominated by the fifty-storey Canada Tower designed by Cesar Pelli. The docklands area of London had been stagnating since the 1960s until it was heavily redeveloped in the 1980s.

# Modern London: 1952–Today

Since World War II, London has seen both good times and bad. In 1954, the food rationing that had come into effect during the war was finally abolished and by the 1960s the city had recovered from the effects of the war and there was a new air of optimism, particularly among the younger generation who flocked to the capital during the latter part of the decade when it became synonymous with the "Swinging Sixties" scene. The look of the city was also beginning to change as high-rise housing, offices, and commercial buildings sprang up. However, some people felt that, as in the wake of the Great Fire of 1666, an opportunity to radically and imaginatively restructure the city was missed due to short-sighted financial and time restraints.

The gloom of the 1970s was followed by economic recovery and regeneration in parts of the city during the 1980s under the Conservative government of Margaret Thatcher. But the policies that led to this recovery also widened the divide between rich and poor. Such was the strength of feeling against the Poll Tax that there was a demonstration against it in Trafalgar Square on March 31, 1990, which turned into a riot lasting into the early hours of the following day. By the end of the year Thatcher, who had personally championed the tax, had resigned and her successor, John Major lost no time in announcing the scrapping of the Poll Tax.

London was seen in a much more positive light on July 13, 1985, when the Live Aid concert organized by Bob Geldof and Midge Ure to raise money for famine relief in Ethiopia was held at Wembley Stadium. Similar events were also held at JFK Stadium, Philadelphia and in Sydney and Moscow. Over 1.5 billion viewers watched the televized event across the world and it would eventually generate around £150 million of aid.

The turn of the century saw the construction of a number of attractions to celebrate the new millennium. Some, such as the London Eye, have been hugely successful and others, such as the Millennium Dome, far less so.

RIGHT: This 620 foot tower was commissioned by the General Post Office and built between 1961 and 1964. Initially it was known as the Post Office Tower and was the tallest building in Britain at that time. When it was originally opened in 1965 there was a rotating restaurant on the thirty-fourth floor, however this has been closed to the public since 1971 when a suspected IRA bomb exploded there. The tower is still operational as a telecommunications mast and is now known as the British Telecom (BT) Tower.

LEFT: During the "Swinging Sixties" London was at the forefront of the explosion in music and fashion. One of the most "hip" streets at the time was Carnaby Street, seen here during Christmas 1967 decked out with pop-art style decorations.

Right: The Royal National Theatre was designed by the architect Sir Denys Lasdun and opened in 1976. Prior to its construction, the National Theatre Company (as it was then known) had been based at the Old Vic since its inception in 1963. The title "Royal" was added in 1988. The building contains three theaters that stage an eclectic mix of old classics and modern plays.

LEFT: The golden-domed London Central Mosque, located on Park Road, on the edge of Regent's Park, was designed by Sir Frederick Gibberd and completed in 1978.

RIGHT: Begun in 1962 and finally completed in 1982, the Barbican complex was built on an area that had been devastated by the air raids of World War II. It combines residential and commercial buildings with artistic venues including two theaters, two cinemas, and a concert hall.

Over the centuries the Thames has flooded on a number of occasions, and in 1965 the Greater London Council invited proposals for a means to alleviate this threat. Work began on the Thames Barrier in 1974 and it was opened in 1984, since when it has been raised on numerous occasions.

LEFT: Built in 1986, the Lloyds building is one of the most striking of London's modern office blocks. Designed by Richard Rogers, it contains echoes of another of his famous works: the Pompidou Center in Paris.

RIGHT: This modern new shopping and office block sits above the platforms of Charing Cross Station. Designed by Terry Farrell it was completed in 1991.

LEFT: Designed by Sir Colin St. John Wilson, the British Library on Euston Road (seen here overlooked by St. Pancras Station) took nearly twenty years to build, finally being opened in 1997. The library holds over sixteen million books and has a copy of virtually every book printed in Britain.

LEFT: The reconstructed Shakespeare's Globe is located on the banks of the River Thames in Southwark. The actor and director Sam Wanamaker who founded the Shakespeare Globe Trust in 1970 was instrumental in its construction. Building work finally began in 1987, but unfortunately Wanamaker died four years before the theater opened in 1997.

ABOVE: The Millennium Dome, situated on a peninsula in Greenwich, has rarely been far from controversy. When it first opened from January 1, 2000 to December 31, 2000, as an exhibition celebrating the beginning of the third millennium it failed to attract the necessary number of visitors. For a long time after this its future was uncertain and though it is now being converted to an indoor sporting arena, its long-term future is still dogged by political controversy.

RIGHT: The magnificent Queen Elizabeth II Great Court in the British Museum was designed by Lord Foster of Thames Bank and was opened by the Queen on December 6, 2000.

The Millennium Bridge was opened
on June 10, 2000. It is a pedestrian-
only concrete and steel suspension
bridge and the first new bridge to be
built across the Thames for over 100
years.

COLLECTION 2002   MATISSE PICASSO   AHTILA

Opened on May 12, 2000, the Tate Modern is housed in the buildings of the old Bankside Power Station. The gallery houses a collection of international modern (post-1900) art and is a part of the Tate group that includes Tate Britain as well as galleries in St. Ives in Cornwall and in Liverpool.

COLLECTION 2002

30 St. Mary Axe, nicknamed "The Gherkin" was designed by Foster and Partners and opened in May 2004. Initially, it was unpopular with Londoners but over time it has become accepted and is now recognized as one of the city's most iconic buildings.

RIGHT: A computer-generated image of the new Wembley Stadium that is due to open in time for the Football Association Cup Final in 2007.

**Picture Credits**

Map page 9: Mark Franklin
All other images from Corbis
2 Kathy Collins; 4–5 Jeremy Horner; 6–7 Murat Taner/zefa; 10 Peter MacDiarmid/Reuters; 11 Fine Art Photographic Library; 13 Historical Picture Archive; 18–19, 41, 52–53, 69, 70–71, 140 Bettmann; 20 Pawel Libera; 22–23 Mike Finn-Kelcey/Files/Reuters; 24–25 Chris North; Cordaiy Photo Library Ltd.; 26–27 Str/epa; 27, 86 Michael Nicholson; 29 Michael Maslan Historic Photographs; 31 Joey Nigh; 32 Angelo Hornak; 33 Simon Warren; 36–37, 44, 60–61 Stapleton Collection; 37 Rune Hellestad; 38–39 Historical Picture Archive; 42 Rupert Horrox; 43, 56, 139 Adam Woolfitt; 45 Historical Picture Archive; 46 John Heseltine; 47, 134–135 Angelo Hornak; 48 Rune Hellestad; 49 PictureNet; 50, 55 Rupert Horrox; 51, 58, 67 (R) Michael Nicholson; 54; 57 Jeremy Horner; 59, 62–63 Dylan Martinez/Files/Reuters; 67 (L) Michael Freeman; 68 Historical Picture Archive; 74–75 Kim Sayer; 76 Massimo Listri; 77 Philippa Lewis; Edifice; 78–79 Gideon Mendel; 80 Michael John Kielty; 81 Geoffrey Taunton; Cordaiy Photo Library Ltd.; 82 Historical Picture Archive; 83 Charles Bowman/Robert Harding World Imagery; 84 (L) Humphrey Evans; Cordaiy Photo Library Ltd.; 84 (R) Angelo Hornak; 85 Carl & Ann Purcell; 87 Graham Tim/Corbis Sygma; 88 Fine Art Photographic Library; 89 Adam Woolfitt; 94–95 image100; 96–97, 99 Massimo Listri; 103 Richard Bryant/Arcaid; 104–105 PictureNet; 106 Roy Rainford/Robert Harding World Imagery; 109 Wolfgang Kaehler; 110, 143 London Aerial Photo Library; 111 Robert Holmes; 112 Image Source; 113 Kim Sayer; 114 Kathy Collins; 115 Free Agents Limited; 117 Peter M. Wilson; 118–119, 148–149, 152–153, 158 Richard Bryant/Arcaid; 119 Martin Jones; 123 Yann Arthus-Bertrand; 124, 128 Kim Sayer; 124–125 WildCountry; 126 Rupert Horrox; 127 Hulton-Deutsch Collection; 129 David Reed; 130–131, 140–141 Pawel Libera; 132–133 Martyn Rose/zefa/Corbis; 136–137 Grant Smith; 152 Toby Melville/Reuters; 144–145; 146 Niall MacLeod; 147 Martin Jones; 150 Jason Hawkes; 151 Reuters; 154–155 Rachel Royse; 156–157 Seamas Culligan/Zuma; 159 London 2012/Handout/Reuters